MAGIC CASTLE READERS®

Little Too-Tall

A book about friendship

BY JANE BELK MONCURE • ILLUSTRATED BY SUSAN DeSANTIS

The Child's World®

Published by The Child's World®
1980 Lookout Drive • Mankato, MN 56003-1705
800-599-READ • www.childsworld.com

Acknowledgments
The Child's World®: Mary Berendes, Publishing Director
The Design Lab: Design
Jody Jensen Shaffer: Editing
Derrick Chow: Color

ISBN 9781623235680
LCCN 2013931410

Printed in the United States of America
Mankato, MN
July 2013
PA02177

Did you know...

A library is a magic castle with many Word Windows in it?

What is a Word Window?

If you said, "A book," you're right!

A book is a Word Window because the words and pictures let you look and see many things. Books are your windows to the wide, wide world around you.

The Library
Is a Magic Castle

Come to the Magic Castle
When you are growing tall.
Rows and rows of Word Windows
Line every single wall.
They reach up high,
As high as the sky,
And you'll want to open them all.
For every time you open one,
A new adventure has begun.

3

Scott opened a Word Window.
Here is what he read:

Little Too-Tall was all alone in the jungle.
"I wish I had a friend," she said.

Just then, a parrot flew by.

"Will you be my friend?" said Little Too-Tall.

"My word," said Parrot.
"You are a funny-looking bird."

"Your legs are too tall. You cannot fly at all.
Good-bye," said Parrot.

Then Little Too-Tall saw a monkey in a tree.
"Will you be my friend?" said Little Too-Tall.

"My word," said Monkey.
"You are a funny-looking bird."

"Your neck is too long. You cannot climb a tree. Good-bye," said Monkey.

A hippo came by on his way for a swim.
"Will you be my friend?" said Little Too-Tall.

"My word," said Hippo.
"You are a funny-looking bird."

"Your eyes are too big. You cannot swim at all."
Good-bye," said Hippo.

"I cannot swim like Hippo or climb like Monkey or fly like Parrot," said Little Too-tall.

"But I can run!" she said. And she did.
Little Too-Tall ran right out of the jungle.

She ran into a grassy field. Far away, Zebra and
Antelope were eating grass.

Little Too-Tall stood very still. Her long neck was high above the grass.

Suddenly, she saw a hungry lion
hiding in the grass.

Little Too-Tall ran past Lion as fast as her tall legs would go.

"Run, Zebra! Run, Antelope!
Run away from Lion!" said Little Too-Tall.

All three ran to safety.

"You saved us from Lion," said Zebra.
"Please stay with us."

"Don't you think I am a funny-looking bird?"
said Little Too-Tall. "My eyes are too big.
My neck is too long. My legs are too tall."

"Not at all," said Antelope. "With your big eyes, your long neck, and your tall legs, you are just the right size."

"You can see Lion when he hides in the grass," said Antelope.

"We like you just the way you are," said Zebra.

"You do?" asked Little Too-Tall.
"Then I will stay."

"We can all be friends," said Antelope and Zebra.

Little Too-Tall laughed a happy laugh
and hopped some happy hops.

Questions and Activities

(Write your answers on a sheet of paper.)

1. Tell this story to a friend. Take only two minutes.
   Which parts did you share?

2. Did parts of this story make you feel sad or happy? Why?

3. Did this story have any words you don't know?
   How can you find out what they mean?

4. Why does Little Too-Tall tell Zebra and Antelope to run?
   Why don't Zebra and Antelope want Little Too-Tall to leave them?

5. In one sentence, tell what this book is about.
   Name three ways the author tells the book's main idea.